THE OFFICIAL

QUEENS PARK RANGERS

ANNUAL 2016

Written by Ian Taylor & Francis Atkinson
Contributions by Matt Webb

Designed by Lucy Boyd

A Grange Publication

© 2015. Published by Grange Communications Ltd., Edinburgh, under licence from Queens Park Rangers Football Club. Printed in the EU.

Photographs © Back Page Images.

ISBN: 9781910199527

WELCOME TO THE OFFICIAL QUEENS PARK RANGERS ANNUAL 2016!

As always this Annual is packed with posters, quizzes, interviews, articles and much, much more! In this year's edition we also look back and celebrate what was arguably QPR's greatest ever side, a team that were pipped by a single point to the title in the 1975/76 campaign.

Enjoy the read

CONTENTS

WELCOMING OUR NEW CLUB AMBASSADOR, ANDY SINTON

The scorer of our first ever Premier League goal and an England international during his time at Loftus Road, Andy Sinton is widely-regarded as one of the club's greatest ever wingers.

A shining light in the R's team that finished as London's top club in 1992/93, Sinton enjoyed some of the finest moments of his career in the Blue and White Hoops.

Things may have – in his own words – "ended rather sourly", but the Newcastle-born wide-man looks back on his time in W12 with nothing but joy and admiration.

In this exclusive interview, Sinton – recently appointed as QPR's first Club Ambassador – lifts the lid on a quite remarkable rise to prominence during his spell with the R's, including tales of the late, great Alan McDonald, his pride at representing his country whilst on QPR's books, and his remarkable relationship with Gerry Francis.

"I lived the dream, it was a dream come true." It's fair to say Andy Sinton looks back on his time as a QPR player with the very highest regard.

Having started his career off as a youngster at Cambridge United, Sinton moved to Brentford in 1985, terrorising lower league defences with his pace and power down the left wing.

He just loved playing football, so when speculation began to circulate in 1989 that QPR were keen on making their move for the Cramlington-born wide-man, he just shrugged it off as another rumour. He was only focused on playing football, nothing more, nothing less.

QPR sent scouts to watch Sinton play for Brentford at Anfield – the home of Liverpool – and the brief was simple: if Sinton performed well against Liverpool right-back and Scotland international Steve Nicol, Rangers would take the plunge.

"I wasn't aware QPR were watching me, but I was aware of there being interest in me," Sinton said.

"QPR, because of their locality, were being linked with me, but I didn't know they'd sent someone to watch me.

"I wasn't worried about people watching me or anything like that. I just wanted to go out there every match and give my best.

"I wanted to play at the highest possible level – that was my motivation, not people watching me."

However, when speculation became fact, and Rangers had a bid accepted for the midfield ace, Sinton jumped at the chance to move across West London to Loftus Road.

"It all came about quite strangely, but I didn't think twice to be honest," says the now 49-year-old.

"We had just played Liverpool and were preparing to play Torquay in the Sherpa Van Trophy or something. Steve Coppell, who was great for me, asked me to stay back for a chat with him after training, which was rare, and I thought it was a bit strange.

"He pulled me into the Boardroom and told me QPR had made an offer, they were keen.

"His advice was that he felt I was good enough to make that step up, even if he didn't want to sell me and the club were under no pressure to let me go.

"He just said, 'I think you're ready to go and test yourself.' He told me to wait by my phone and in those days you didn't have a mobile, so I stayed at the club.

"I eventually got a call later that day saying the clubs had agreed everything and I spoke to Trevor (Francis). I went to his house at Wentworth on the golf course, a lovely place.

"We spoke about why he wanted me at the club. We spoke at length and I had no hesitations in joining a club two leagues up the pyramid.

"I had high aspirations as a player and believed in my own ability. I thought I was ready, so there was no pressure – it was a dream come true."

Sinton made a fast start to life in W12, making his debut in a 2-0 win against Sheffield Wednesday before scoring on his home bow at Loftus Road versus Aston Villa a few days later.

Looking back, he admits it couldn't have gone much better.

"I always remember a journalist asking me on the day I signed, 'How long do you think it will be before you get in the QPR first team?' Being quite cocky at the time, I said, 'two days!' He replied, 'Why's that?' and I said, 'Well we're playing away to Sheffield Wednesday at the weekend and I expect to play!'

"I always had faith in my own ability and Trevor put me straight in there on the wing. We went up to Hillsborough and won 2-0. Then I scored the winner against Aston Villa in my home debut a few days later. So I more or less established myself straight away in the Rangers side."

He added, "A goal and a win on my home debut was remarkable. The stuff of dreams.

"I've still got a copy of that goal on DVD. I still remember it as if it was yesterday.

"It was the 71st minute, on a bobbly pitch and the corner came over in front of the Loft, 1-0.

"It was a great way to introduce myself to the QPR fans. I wouldn't say I had the greatest game in the world, but it was nice to score the winner, get the club three valuable points, and to have back-to-back wins after beating Sheffield Wednesday.

"Those two wins went some way to ensuring we stayed in the league. We stayed up comfortably in the end, but at that stage it looked very touch and go."

Despite flourishing under Trevor Francis, it was under the guidance of his namesake, Gerry, that Sinton really began to hit new heights.

His arrival in the summer of 1991 saw Rangers go from strength to strength, as Sinton acknowledged.

"Gerry, without doubt, had the biggest impact on me," he said.

"I count myself extremely lucky, blessed, fortunate that I played for some really good managers, and I'm often asked the question about who was the best.

"Gerry had a massive impact on me because of the nature of my career – climbing the ladder from Brentford to QPR and then to an England call-up within 18 months.

"I remember the first time I sat in front of him and he told me he thought I was a fantastic player, which is always great to hear! He made it clear that he felt if I kept doing what I was doing, performing to the best of my ability, that I could go on to represent England.

"I was embarrassed to be honest, but he believed in me and kept on reaffirming that message, and through hard work and determination I got there.

"Maybe it was Gerry's way. His gift was taking people like me – and Les – from being good players to better players.

"He certainly believed in me and kept telling me the right things, and in QPR I had an incredible environment to showcase my talents.

"We weren't the most fashionable of clubs back then, but he made the place feel very homely. There was a fantastic spirit in the club and Gerry created that.

"We all worked incredibly hard, and possibly over-achieved, but Gerry was brilliant. Brilliant for me, brilliant for everyone in that team. Everyone spoke highly about him and I have so much to thank him for."

Prior to the 1991/92 season kicking off, QPR received £1.75million from Manchester United for England defender Paul Parker. Later that season, a further £1million saw Ray Wegerle depart for Blackburn Rovers.

However, the unity of the squad remained and one of a number of fine displays that season saw them thrash Manchester United on their own patch at Old Trafford.

In front of 38,554 spectators – and a live television audience – the R's ran the Red Devils ragged to win 4-1, with Dennis Bailey hitting a hat-trick.

Sinton scored the first on that evening at the Theatre of Dreams and it goes down as one of the highlights of his career.

"To go to Man Utd. on New Year's Day and come away winning 4-1, live on the TV – it doesn't get much better than that," Sinton said.

"I remember I scored the first after four or five minutes, then Dennis got his first a few minutes later and you think, 'Wow, we could win here'.

"I actually had a really good feeling before the game. I remember we were in a wine bar the night before seeing in the New Year with half a lager – Gerry was good like that and no-one abused their position. We raised a glass, and when we went back to the room I remember saying to Simon Barker, who I roomed with, that I had a really positive feeling about us.

"The rest is history – but what a game, what a memory."

He added: "Any player that goes to Manchester United and wins 4-1 and puts on a good show – you come away feeling really good about yourself and the team.

"We knew we were a good side though. We knew we had good players and we knew on our day we were a match for anyone. We were starting to find a good level of consistency.

"Team spirit will only take you so far. Ability with no team spirit will only take you so far. We had a little bit of everything.

"We weren't the greatest team, but we worked hard for each other. We were proud to pull on the shirt and gave everything every time we crossed the white line.

"From a personal point of view, I never looked too far ahead. I was just a kid from Newcastle living the dream. I had a wonderful family, great kids and great team-mates at a great club – it was just a privilege."

The R's finished 11th in the league that season, ensuring their place in the new FA Premier League for the next season.

Sinton, as you'd expect, made an immediate impact, scoring the R's first-ever Premier League goal against Manchester City on the first-ever Sky Sports Monday Night Football.

Trailing to David White's 37th minute opener, Sinton and Rangers hit back shortly after half-time to claim a deserved share of the spoils.

Controlling the ball expertly on his chest, Sinton took one touch to set himself before firing an unstoppable left-footed strike from fully 25 yards into the roof of the net to put Rangers on terms.

"That goal will always be special," he said.

"It was from 25 yards or so – and as the years go by it gets further and further out by the way!

"From an individual point of view, it was always nice to score on the television and it was a good goal. I cut inside and shot into the top corner so it was particularly pleasing.

"That started us off on a really fine season in the Premier League. Not just for myself, but for everyone at QPR as we finished as top London club."

Rangers went on to finish fifth that season, with Les Ferdinand hitting a remarkable 20 goals thanks in kind to Sinton, who struck up an excellent on-the-field relationship with his England team-mate.

"We knew we were becoming a good side that was hard to beat," recalls Sinton.

"We knew from going on international duty and speaking to our fellow professionals that teams didn't like coming to QPR. Loftus Road is a wonderful stadium – so it's intimidating when the crowd are in full voice.

"When there's a big club in town, that's when Rangers fans really find their voice. We beat a lot of top sides because of the twelfth man playing their part.

"It was great – we knew we were on to something good, because we knew we had a togetherness, a team spirit, and a group of players with good ability.

"I never really thought about how far we could go, but I knew we had the quality to keep improving.

"I was just focused on playing every week, doing the job I was getting paid for – it was all that mattered. I loved every minute."

On his relationship with Ferdinand, Sinton's face lights up as he recalls the on-the-field bond the pair shared.

He recalls a "great player" and "great lad", with whom he shared an incredible understanding.

"People used to say we had a great understanding and we did," he said.

"Gerry just used to encourage me to hit an area and Les would make an okay cross into a really good one.

"He was phenomenal in the air, had great pace and what I would say about Les is that he was the difference.

"We had a lot of good players, but he was the tipping point. Like in all good sides, Les could get you something out of nothing.

"Allied to all the other good players we had in that side, he was the star."

Another team-mate Sinton held in extremely high regard was Ray Wilkins. A godparent to one of his children, the duo struck up an instant rapport.

"I can't speak highly enough of Ray. We got on really well, still do," he said.

"He was a fantastic player. I remember when he signed at the age of 34 with 80 England caps, having played for some of Europe's top clubs and – forgive me for saying this – I thought 'Has he come back to London for the right reasons?'

"But from the first day he walked in the door, he was incredible. He never missed a day's training. He was always leading from the front.

"Someone once told me you have to play with players to understand just how good they are – Ray Wilkins was one of those players. He was phenomenal.

"He was great with people like me and Les, telling us to believe in ourselves.

"He treated everyone within the club – and outside – wonderfully.

"As a human being he had an incredible impact on me – how to conduct yourself, how to act, speak, look. He was incredible, a wonderful, wonderful team-mate and friend."

During his time at Loftus Road, Sinton burst into the full England team and eventually went on to win 12 caps.

From his debut against Poland in November 1991, to his last England cap versus San Marino in a 7-1 rout two years later, he was delighted to represent his country.

"My England debut was the highlight of my career, without a doubt," he said.

"The proudest moment of my career was standing in Poland for my debut on a freezing cold November night and the national anthem started playing.

"I tried to sing but I couldn't because I was just so choked. Everything was flashing through my mind.

"From being eight years-old and playing on the streets where I grew up, pretending to be an England player, for that to become a reality – I still have to pinch myself today.

"I'm a really proud Englishman. I love to see the national side do well.

"I know the game has changed these days, but when I hear of international players pulling out of the squad and missing friendlies then it does annoy me a little bit. I gave everything on every single occasion I played for England. And I felt it was also a reflection on my club and the supporters, and so I felt proud for them too.

"I was really proud to represent QPR on

England duty, because without QPR, I wouldn't have played for the Three Lions.

"I grew up wanting to pull that white shirt on – it was a dream come true. I felt really blessed."

After a fine four-year spell in which he made 161 league starts, scoring 22 goals, Sinton left QPR for Sheffield Wednesday in a £2.75m deal in August 1993.

He is keen to assure supporters he never did anything to initiate his controversial transfer to Hillsborough.

Whereas David Seaman and Paul Parker had joined Arsenal and Manchester United respectively, Sinton's 'sideways' move to Wednesday was badly received.

"I was saddened by how it all ended," he said.

"There was a myth that I'd asked to leave. I didn't – I was very happy at QPR and had no reason to leave.

"There was this perception that I broke into the England side and then decided I wanted to go. That's not the truth.

"When you're away with your country, you talk to different people from different clubs and you get to hear what player X is earning. After a while, when you know that you're a better player and give more, you start to think.

"When I came home after that England tour, I told Gerry I thought I deserved X amount in terms of my salary. I think Gerry was probably in agreement but the club couldn't do it and within a week or so I was told to speak to other clubs.

"Maybe looking back, it was on the cards because QPR were a selling club – Seaman, (Roy) Wegerle, Parker, Ferdinand.

"And the week before I went, Trevor Sinclair was signed and went straight into my positon."

He added, "All I will say is that my time at QPR was the best of my career. I loved the club, we'd just finished London's top club, so there wasn't a great deal to move away for.

"In those days there weren't mobile phones, so I don't know what was said. The perception was that I tried to engineer a move away. That wasn't right.

"If QPR would have come up with somewhere near the deal I wanted, I would have stayed. People might say 'Well you didn't have to go' but the club didn't have to sell me either.

"So it all ended a little bit sourly for me.

"I remember coming back on New Year's Day with Sheffield Wednesday and I took a bit of stick and that really, really hurt me. It took me by surprise. I wasn't expecting it.

"I guess people were fed a certain line and believed it. I never really gave my side of the story, but that's how it goes sometime.

"It could have been handled a little bit better, but life moves on. I left under a cloud, but people ask me where I was happiest at in my career – QPR, make no mistake about it."

Now a new chapter has been opened, with Sinton's role as Club Ambassador bringing him back to the place he calls "home."

SPOT THE BALL

QPR's Tjaronn Chery strikes a lovely free-kick during the home pre-season friendly with Atalanta of Italy, but can you spot the ball?

Answer on page 60-61

CHAMPIONS FOR TEN DAYS

The story of QPR's famous 1975/76 First Division title push – 40 seasons on …

Unquestionably the greatest season in the history of Queens Park Rangers Football Club, 1975/76, saw the R's come oh-so-close to First Division championship glory.

Boss Dave Sexton's brand of free-flowing football wooed the Loftus Road faithful. On the very first day of the season Gerry Francis set the tone for the rest of the campaign with a goal-of-the-year effort, created thanks to a wonderful team move.

That particular strike helped Rangers to a 2-0 opening day win over Liverpool. We may not have known it at the time, but the Anfield men would eventually pip us to the title.

On the road, things began in equally impressive fashion. Rangers won 5-1 against reigning champions Derby County, with Stan Bowles getting a hat-trick. Derby were the third national champions QPR had beaten within a month, following comprehensive pre-season triumphs over Borussia Mönchengladbach (Germany) and Benfica (Portugal).

An impressive start for his club saw Gerry Francis named England captain. Rangers, meanwhile, continued to flourish and after home wins over Manchester United and Leicester City, we sailed to the summit of England's top division for the very first time in our history.

After another win at home to Newcastle United, the Hoops lost their first match 2-1 to Leeds United. We bounced straight back with a 5-0 hammering of Everton. Rangers were knocked off the top by a 2-0 defeat at Burnley, but returned to pole position the following week with a 1-0 win over Sheffield United.

Three successive draws saw QPR drop down to fourth place. But two home wins and two draws saw us back on top at the halfway point of the season. We had 28 points from 21 fixtures and had lost only two games.

The year ended badly with three away defeats in four games. The only success was on Boxing Day against Norwich City. Another away defeat followed by a home win kept Rangers in fifth place.

The next game saw the start of one of the best periods in the club's history. Rangers gained 23 points from the next 24 available, thanks to 11 victories and one draw between January 31st and April 10th. The run started with a 2-0 win at Aston Villa and was followed by a 4-2 home success over Wolverhampton Wanderers.

A 3-0 win at Tottenham Hotspur moved Rangers up to third, and a week later we were second after a 2-0 home victory over

QUEENS PARK RANGERS F.C. 1975/76

Back Row: Don Rogers, John Beck, Don Givens, Tommy Cunningham, Keith Pritchett, Danny Westwood, Dave Thomas.
Middle Row: Stan Bowles, Don Shanks, Martyn Busby, Richard Teale, Phil Parkes, Ron Abbott, Mick Leach, Ian Gillard.
Front Row: Dave Webb, Frank McLintock, Dave Clement, Gerry Francis (Club Captain), John Hollins, Don Masson.

Ipswich Town. The next two games, both away, saw a 1-0 win at Leicester City and the only point dropped with a 0-0 draw at Sheffield United.

The R's reached the top of the league again with a resounding 4-1 win at home against Coventry City. Two more away victories followed, 2-0 at Everton and 1-0 at Stoke City. Rangers were a point clear of Manchester United and two clear of Liverpool, but had played a game more. After a 1-0 home win over Manchester City and a 2-1 away success at Newcastle United the Hoops were still on top. By now, we had guaranteed ourselves a place in Europe for the following campaign.

On April 10th, QPR won 4-2 at home to Middlesbrough. Results elsewhere meant that if Rangers won their three remaining games they would be league champions regardless. We had one away game and two home fixtures to come.

On Easter Saturday, Rangers were at Norwich City and a large number of fans made the trip to Carrow Road. The match was a very tense affair. Both sides scored once before half-time, but disaster struck in the second half when Norwich went on to win it. Despite all our efforts, QPR could not equalise.

Our players and fans were more disheartened when the news came through

from Anfield that Liverpool had beaten Stoke City 5-2. QPR now had to win their two remaining home games and hope that Liverpool would lose one of their two remaining away fixtures.

Rangers beat Arsenal on Easter Monday, but Liverpool also won 3-0 at Manchester City. On the last Saturday of the season the R's were at home to Leeds United, but Liverpool didn't play due to international commitments.

We beat Leeds United 2-0 in front of our largest gate of the season, 31,002. This meant that Rangers had finished their games and were top of the league. Now a 10-day wait ensued to see how Liverpool would do against the relegation-threatened Wolves.

At half-time Wolves led through a John Richards goal. They held on until 13 minutes from time when Kevin Keegan equalised. When the news came through that Birmingham had won and Wolves could not stay up, the fight went out of them. Liverpool scored twice more to win 3-1 and take the title in dramatic fashion.

A sorry end for Rangers, but what a campaign.

Read on and learn more about that celebrated side of '75/76, as well as the 'team behind the team.'

1975/76 PLAYER PROFILES

RON ABBOTT – MIDFIELDER
APPEARANCES: 54, GOALS: 4

Midfielder Ron Abbott made a fine start to life at QPR, scoring the winning goal on his first-team debut versus West Ham United in a First Division fixture in September 1973. Often used from the substitutes' bench, Abbott was a dependable deputy who made a total of 54 appearances for QPR, scoring four goals.

JOHN BECK – MIDFIELDER
APPEARANCES: 47, GOALS: 1

Set-piece specialist John Beck was a fine crosser of the football. He is also well-known for his managerial exploits. In 1990, Beck took Cambridge United to the FA Cup quarter-finals and to the brink of the Premier League in 1992. He has also gone on to manage Preston North End and Lincoln City, among other teams.

STAN BOWLES – FORWARD
APPEARANCES: 315, GOALS: 97

Stanley Bowles – one of the greatest players that's ever pulled on the famous blue and white hoops. Many argue that the former number 10 is the best. Born in Manchester, he was a supremely gifted striker who joined from Carlisle United in 1972. His tally of 11 goals in the 1976/77 UEFA Cup run was a record for any Football League player in European competition. He won five England caps during his time with QPR, but left for Nottingham Forest in December 1979.

MARTYN BUSBY – MIDFIELDER
APPEARANCES: 72, GOALS: 14

Martyn Busby was involved in QPR's squad throughout the 1970s. In total he made 72 appearances in midfield for the R's and scored 14 goals. Severe injury ended his career in 1980 before he went into pub management. Busby was later named Beaconsfield United boss.

DAVE CLEMENT – DEFENDER
APPEARANCES: 476, GOALS: 27

Born in Battersea, Dave Clement was an impressive right-back who came up through the ranks at Loftus Road to make close to 500 appearances. He transferred to Bolton Wanderers in June 1979 after claiming five England caps. Clement tragically took his own life in 1982, aged only 34.

GERRY FRANCIS – MIDFIELDER
APPEARANCES: 356, GOALS: 72

Gerry Francis – QPR's ex-midfielder and manager – is one of our most famous former crowd favourites. Francis captained England and won 12 caps as a Rangers player. Born in Chiswick on December 6th 1951, he came up through the youth ranks at Loftus Road and made his debut as a substitute versus Liverpool on March 29th 1969. Francis made 356 appearances for the R's in two spells and scored 72 times, including the BBC goal of the season in 1975/76 (also against Liverpool). He later managed Rangers twice, masterminding a top-five finish in the first season of the Premier League in 1992/93, and is now on the coaching staff at West Bromwich Albion.

IAN GILLARD – DEFENDER
APPEARANCES: 485, GOALS: 11

One of the longer-serving players in our history, left-back Ian Gillard was an ever-present in 1975/76 – and a consistently good one too. A local lad born in Hammersmith on October 9th 1950, Gillard came up through the youth ranks at Loftus Road before making his first-team debut against Nottingham Forest on November 23rd 1968. He made a total of 485 appearances for Rangers, scoring 11 times, and won three England caps as a QPR player. He appeared for us in the 1982 FA Cup final before being transferred to Aldershot later that summer. Gillard has since worked in a confectionery factory and has also run his own cleaning business.

DON GIVENS – STRIKER
APPEARANCES: 294, GOALS: 100

The son of a champion jockey hurdler, Don Givens excelled in a different sport altogether. The forward was a potent finisher and very mobile. He was also a fantastic header of the football and top scorer for us in 1975/76. Born in Limerick on August 9th 1949, Givens signed from Luton Town for £40,000 in July 1972. He made 294 appearances for the R's, scoring 100 goals. He won 27 of his 56 Republic of Ireland caps as a QPR player, hitting a hat-trick against Russia and four versus Turkey. Givens transferred to Birmingham City in August 1978 for £150,000 and is now on the Eire international scouting staff.

JOHN HOLLINS – MIDFIELDER
APPEARANCES: 183, GOALS: 7

A former player and coach for QPR, John Hollins was an elegant midfielder in our great team of the mid-1970s. Hollins appeared 183 times for the R's and scored seven goals. He later returned to Loftus Road on the coaching staff and was caretaker manager in November/December 1997.

MICK LEACH – MIDFIELDER
APPEARANCES: 361, GOALS: 70

Hard-working midfielder Mick Leach made over 350 appearances for the R's, scoring an impressive 70 goals for us in the process. Former boss Alec Stock first brought Leach into the team, and his inclusion coincided with promotion to the First Division in 1967/68. Leach's stay at Loftus Road lasted 14 years in total. He moved to America in 1978, but soon returned to play for Cambridge United before appearing on the non-league scene.

DON MASSON – MIDFIELDER
APPEARANCES: 144, GOALS: 24

Don Masson was a fine passer of the ball who played alongside Gerry Francis in our title challenge team of 1975/76. Born in Banchory, Scotland on August 26th 1946, he signed from Notts County for £100,000 in December 1974. He played 144 times for QPR, scoring 24 goals. Masson won 14 of his 17 Scotland caps while at Loftus Road and transferred to Derby County in exchange for Leighton James in October 1977. He now owns a hotel in the Midlands.

FRANK MCLINTOCK – DEFENDER
APPEARANCES: 163, GOALS: 6

After joining QPR at the veteran stage of his career, Frank McLintock's defensive nous helped QPR challenge Liverpool for the 1975/76 title. Born on December 28th 1939 in Glasgow, Scotland, McLintock joined from Arsenal in June 1973 for £30,000. He was previously the league and FA Cup double-winning captain for the Gunners, won nine Scottish international caps and was awarded an MBE. McLintock went on to play 163 times for the R's and scored six goals. He retired from playing in 1977. McLintock subsequently managed Leicester City and Brentford, and then worked as a pundit for Sky TV. He is now a director of a security firm in London.

PHIL NUTT – STRIKER
APPEARANCES: 4, GOALS: 1

Phil Nutt played few games for the R's, just four in fact, with injury cruelly ending his career extremely early. Nutt netted the equaliser in a 1-1 home draw with Derby County during 1975/76. He debuted in November 1975 versus Stoke City at Loftus Road (QPR won 3-2).

TONY TAGG – DEFENDER
APPEARANCES: 4, GOALS: 0

Central defender Tony Tagg made his debut in our 5-1 trouncing of then-First Division champions Derby County at the Baseball Ground in 1975/76. The stopper only made four appearances in total for us. He is best remembered for his time at Millwall, for whom he played over 100 games.

PHIL PARKES – GOALKEEPER
APPEARANCES: 406

Famed for that trademark 'tache alongside his goalkeeping prowess, Phil Parkes was QPR's number one during the 1975/76 title challenge. He is one of our great goalkeepers from the past. Born in Sedgley, West Midlands on August 8th 1950, Parkes joined us from Walsall in June 1970 for £15,000. He went on to make 406 appearances for QPR and won one England cap. A world record goalkeeper transfer fee of £565,000 took him to West Ham United in February 1979. Parkes now runs his own building firm in Berkshire.

DAVE THOMAS – MIDFIELDER
APPEARANCES: 220, GOALS: 34

First signed by Gordon Jago, flamboyant winger Dave Thomas was a major component of the side that was agonisingly denied title glory at the death. Thomas was born in Kirkby on October 5th 1950 and he joined the R's from Burnley in October 1972 for £165,000. The two-footed midfielder played 220 times for QPR in all and hit 34 goals. Thomas also won eight England caps in his time at Loftus Road. He transferred to Everton for £200,000 in August 1977 and has now retired after working as a PE teacher at a school in Sussex.

DON SHANKS – DEFENDER
APPEARANCES: 206, GOALS: 11

Right-back Don Shanks joined QPR from Luton Town for £35,000 in November 1974. It took the defender time to break into the side but once he did, Shanks was rarely missing for Rangers. He helped the Hoops to First Division second place in 1975/76 and made 206 appearances for us in all, netting 11 goals. Spells at Brighton & Hove Albion and various continental sides followed thereafter.

DAVE WEBB – DEFENDER
APPEARANCES: 146, GOALS: 14

Dave Webb was an imposing figure at centre-half in our legendary team of the mid-1970s. Webb originally joined Rangers from Chelsea in July 1974 for £120,000. He went on to make 147 appearances in a hooped shirt and scored 11 goals before eventually moving on to Leicester City in September 1977 in a £50,000 transfer.

1975/76 STAFF PROFILES

DAVE SEXTON – MANAGER
QPR BOSS: 1974-77

Forward-thinking boss Dave Sexton almost brought First Division title success to QPR after the team adopted a continental approach. Sexton would often fly abroad on his days off to watch other teams play, and Rangers' brand of free-flowing play saw us win many fans outside of Loftus Road. In 1974, the former West Ham United, Leyton Orient and Brighton & Hove Albion player was appointed manager at Loftus Road just 13 days after being sacked by local rivals Chelsea. After finishing second in 1975/76, Rangers reached the quarter-finals of the UEFA Cup in 1977. QPR also made the League Cup semis in the same year and Sexton was lured away with a move to Manchester United.

FRANK SIBLEY – ASSISTANT MANAGER
APPEARANCES: 168, GOALS: 5
QPR BOSS: 1977-78 & 1984-85

After debuting as a player for us at the age of just 15 years and 275 days old, severe injury unfortunately forced Frank Sibley into early retirement in 1974. Former defender Sibley played in our 1967 League Cup final win over West Bromwich Albion at Wembley. He was promoted to first-team manager in 1977 after the departure of Dave Sexton to Manchester United. After resigning in 1978, he enjoyed a brief spell in charge once more in 1984/85.

RON PHILLIPS – CLUB SECRETARY / PROGRAMME EDITOR

Ron Phillips was QPR club secretary and programme editor from 1966 right up until 1989, completing over 20 years of service. He helped create our famous old programme cover with multi-coloured squares and stickmen, and his Bush Telegraph notes were both interesting and punchy. He now runs a theatre in west London.

SHEILA MARSON – ASSISTANT CLUB SECRETARY

Sheila Marson has a long association with QPR after over 30 years of service. She previously held a role at Chelsea Football Club. Marson would go on to become our club secretary. Still held in high regard by former work colleagues and fans alike, she continues to be a frequent visitor to Loftus Road in the present day.

MICHAEL WALE – PROGRAMME CONTRIBUTOR

Former programme contributor Michael Wale also worked in local radio and television while helping the club. Wale conducted player interviews for the programme and still works in the media today.

GORDON JAGO – FORMER MANAGER
QPR BOSS: 1971-74

The foundations for success in 1975/76 were laid, to a degree, by ex-boss Gordon Jago. The former Charlton Athletic player took over as manager from Les Allen, to whom he was assistant. Despite Rodney Marsh leaving for Manchester City, Jago took QPR to the First Division in 1973, and eighth position the next season. He became Millwall manager until 1978 before emigrating to America, where he has held various posts since.

With thanks to Gordon Macey and Tony Incenzo

2014/15 PLAYER OF THE YEAR AWARDS

For the second year running, Charlie Austin dominated QPR's end-of-season awards at the end of the 2014/15 season.

The R's striker – who scored an incredible 18 Premier League goals in his maiden season in the top flight – was voted Supporters' Player of the Year.

He was also named Ray Jones Players' Player of the Year, with his team-mates acknowledging his fantastic contribution in what was ultimately a disappointing campaign for the club.

The striker also collected the Junior Hoops' Player of the Year accolade.

Darnell Furlong was named the Daphne Biggs Young Player of the Year, as voted for by the R's fans, following a season that saw him break into the QPR first team.

Having not played a professional fixture prior to this season, the right-back made three appearances for the R's this term.

Meanwhile, Matt Phillips won the Kiyan Prince Goal of the Season award for his outrageous 43-yard thunderbolt against Crystal Palace at Selhurst Park in March.

Chris Kemp was voted Supporter of the Year by his fellow fans for the backing he has shown the club through the years. Chris has attended more than 1,250 consecutive QPR matches home and away.

RAY JONES
PLAYERS' PLAYER OF
THE YEAR
**CHARLIE
AUSTIN**

SUPPORTERS'
PLAYER OF
THE YEAR
**CHARLIE
AUSTIN**

21

KIYAN PRINCE
GOAL OF
THE SEASON
MATT
PHILLIPS

SUPPORTER
OF THE YEAR
CHRIS
KEMP

JUNIOR
HOOPS' PLAYER
OF THE YEAR
CHARLIE
AUSTIN

QUIZ: PART ONE

1 Who was QPRs leading goalscorer in the 2014/15 season? How many league goals did he score?

....

2 Name the two Chilean internationals on loan during the last campaign?

....

3 How many own goals did QPR concede during the 2014/15 season?

....

4 Who notched the Rangers' first goal of the season last year?

....

5 Against whom was our first Premier League win of the 2014/15 season, and by what scoreline?

....

6 Which England international played the most minutes on the pitch for QPR during the 2014/15 season?

....

7 Which QPR player made the most assists in 2014/15?

....

8 Which ex-Manchester United defender did QPR sign at the beginning of the 2014/15 campaign? Which squad number did he take?

....

9 Who wore the Rangers famous number 10 shirt during the 2014/15 season, and which country does he represent?

....

10 Who took over as QPR manager after Harry Redknapp's resignation?

....

11 How many players made their QPR first team debuts during the 2014/15 Premier League campaign?

....

12 Who was the Rangers' first choice penalty-taker? And how many did he subsequently score and miss over the course of the 2014/15 season?

....

13 How many red cards did the Super Hoops notch up during the season?

....

14 Which shirt number was famously worn by Rangers' current Director of Football? Can you name the R's Director of Football?

....

15 Against which team did we achieve our highest Loftus Road attendance in 2014/15?

....

16 Which son of a former Rangers legend made his first team debut at right-back, and against which side?

....

17 Throughout the 2014/15 season, how many league goals did the Rangers score?

....

18 What was the R's highest victory, and against whom?

....

19 Which national team does winger Matty Phillips represent?

....

20 Which Super Hoops attacking midfielder enjoyed his second loan spell at the club during the 2014/15 season?

....

Answers on page 60-61

THE MANAGEMENT TEAM

It was another busy period of change at Loftus Road in 2015, with R's legend Les Ferdinand taking on a new role as Director of Football. Chris Ramsey was appointed Head Coach on a full-time basis at the end of the 2014/15 season, whilst popular Rangers man Steve Gallen was promoted into the First Team coaching set-up over the summer. Here, we take a look at the trio's careers to date.

LES FERDINAND – DIRECTOR OF FOOTBALL

Les Ferdinand is a man who needs no introduction to QPR fans, young and old. Those of a certain vintage will remember only too fondly the goals 'Sir Les' scored for the club in the top flight, while the younger generation will have heard many a story about our famous Number 9.

Before Ferdinand wrote his name into the folklore of QPR, he began his career playing non-league football with Hayes.

In March 1987, aged 20, the powerful and rapid front man completed a move to Loftus Road for a reported £15,000.

In his early days in W12, Ferdinand struggled to adapt to life in England's top division and spent time on loan with Besiktas (twice) and Brentford. Despite an impressive season with the Turkish side, Ferdinand still found first-team opportunities difficult to come by at QPR. He looked set to be leaving the club before Gerry Francis arrived as manager in the summer of 1991.

In the Premier League's inaugural season, Ferdinand hit 20 league goals to help Rangers finish fifth. He followed that up with another 40 league goals in the next two seasons before he joined Newcastle for £6million – a 40,000% mark-up on his arrival fee!

In total, Ferdinand scored 90 goals in 183 appearances in all competitions for QPR before his move to St James' Park in the summer of 1995.

An impressive 50 goals in just two seasons with Newcastle led Tottenham to pay another

£6million for his services, and he would spend the next seven years with the north London side.

Injuries limited his playing time during this period, but he still racked up another 33 goals in all competitions.

Ferdinand enjoyed spells with West Ham, Leicester, Bolton and Reading before retiring in 2006.

He is part of an elite club of players to have scored more than 100 Premier League goals. Currently, he is the eighth highest scorer in the competition's history, with 149 goals.

Internationally, Ferdinand represented England on 17 occasions, scoring five goals.

After hanging up his playing boots, Ferdinand spent six years on the coaching staff at Spurs before leaving the club in the summer of 2014.

HEAD COACH – CHRIS RAMSEY

After coming through the ranks at Bristol City, Ramsey went on to play for Brighton, Swindon and Southend, predominantly as a right-back.

During his spell with the Seagulls, Ramsey played in the 1983 FA Cup Final against Manchester United, which finished goalless. Injury ruled him out of the replay, which Brighton lost 4-0.

While at Swindon, Ramsey won back-to-back promotions. In 1986, the Robins won the Fourth Division title, and the following season they were promoted from the Third Division after beating Gillingham in the Play-Off Final.

In 1988, Ramsey combined his playing career with a coaching role when he moved to Naxxar Lions in Malta. After three years, he headed to Florida where he represented Cocoa Expos as a player, assistant coach and coach.

In 1998, Ramsey joined the FA as Regional Director of Coaching before working as England Under-20 head coach. He also worked as assistant coach for the England Under-16s.

In 2004, Ramsey joined Tottenham where he worked as Head of Player Development, and he eventually operated as a First Team Coach before leaving White Hart Lane in 2014 after ten years with the club.

Ramsey joined QPR in November 2014 as Head of Player Development and Academy Manager. Following Harry Redknapp's resignation in February 2015, Ramsey was placed in caretaker charge of first team affairs before being appointed as the club's new Head Coach in May 2015.

FIRST TEAM COACH –
STEVE GALLEN

Steve Gallen was appointed QPR youth development manager in 2009, following a number of years in charge of the R's Under-16 squad.

Gallen, who grew up in Acton, West London, captained Rangers' Youth Team early in his career, but was released after a series of injuries.

Despite this, Gallen joined Yorkshire outfit Doncaster Rovers before spells in the Far East and non-league football.

Gallen also represented Republic of Ireland at Under-18 and Under-21 level.

After completing his coaching badges he began work with the R's Under-10 squad.

Gallen, along with previous Elite Development Squad manager Marc Bircham, took temporary charge of QPR's first team in December 2009.

His Under-18 side were crowned Professional Development League Two Champions following their play-off final win over Huddersfield Town last season.

Bircham's departure to Millwall in January 2014 paved the way for Gallen's appointment as Under-21s Head Coach, taking the reins on a permanent basis a month later.

Gallen guided Rangers youngsters to the Professional Development League Two Play-Off Final that year and was appointed as First Team Coach 12 months later following the exit of Kevin Bond.

THE CAPTAIN

Nedum Onuoha will lead QPR in the 2015/16 season.

The 28-year-old, who prior to this season had made 98 appearances for the club, was handed the armband by Chris Ramsey for the new SkyBet Championship campaign.

Speaking exclusively to www.qpr.co.uk, Onuoha expressed his delight – and surprise – at being handed the role and admits he is relishing the opportunity to lead the R's, commenting, "It's a real honour and a privilege.

"Was it a surprise? Yes it was.

"I think it was Pele that said that he never wanted to be captain, but he wanted to be a leader on the pitch. I've always tried to be that person, but to have the official title now feels great.

"I'm very close to all the players and can pretty much speak to anyone.

"I'm not a youngster anymore and I've been here three years, so I know the club and the way things work here.

"I'm really pleased and relishing the challenge that the role will bring."

Ramsey believes Onuoha's professionalism and leadership skills, combined with his defensive qualities, make him the ideal candidate for the role.

"I've been so impressed with Nedum in my short time here and I firmly believe he is the right man to lead us next season," he said.

"He's a leader on and off the pitch and a great ambassador for this club in terms of the way he goes about his business.

"His professionalism is second to none, and combined with what he brings to us on the pitch, he is real captain's material.

"Clint (Hill) will continue as club captain. In him and Nedum, we have two men who have the full respect of their team-mates and supporters, and are a huge part of the QPR family."

QUIZ: PART TWO – KITS

1 Name the two finals in which QPR have worn an all-white kit?

....

2 What colour was the very first shirt that QPR ever played in?

....

3 When QPR wore their first ever hooped shirt, what colour were the hoops?

....

4 The club had Guinness as shirt sponsors between which years?

....

5 What colour kit did QPR play in during the 1982 FA Cup final?

....

6 Which company made the QPR kit between the years 1997-2007?

....

7 What was the name of QPR's own-branded shirt?

....

8 What is unusual about the kit in this action picture of full-back Ian Gillard?

....

9 What was the make of the QPR kit in our famous 1975/76 season?

....

10 Who was the manufacturer of the kit when the red pin stripe, adjacent to the blue hoops, first appeared?

....

11 Name four airlines that have had their names across the front of QPR shirts.

....

12 In which year did we first wear blue and white hoops?

....

13 Name the QPR kit manufacturer in the image.

....

14 The shirt sponsor between 1996 and 2001 shares its name with an ex-England manager, can you name it?

....

15 In 1992/93 the R's were sponsored by which famous radio station?

....

16 In 1990/91 QPR had a third kit sponsored by Influence that they never played in. What colour was that shirt?

....

17 How many years were QPR in partnership with kit manufacturer Adidas?

....

18 What are the average number of hoops worn by QPR on the kit over the years?

....

19 What colour hoops were re-introduced as a third kit in 1991/92?

....

20 What was the first year that a sponsor appeared on a QPR kit? Can you name the sponsor?

....

Answers on page 60-61

WORDSEARCH: THEN

Find the words in the grid. Words can go horizontally, vertically and diagonally in all eight directions.

S	A	D	W	N	O	T	X	E	S	L	K
N	B	Y	R	E	X	B	S	N	E	L	C
E	B	K	S	N	B	N	O	A	N	L	Q
V	O	W	R	I	I	B	C	W	E	T	R
I	T	K	D	L	C	H	Z	M	L	Y	M
G	T	G	L	K	X	N	E	N	B	E	A
T	H	O	M	A	S	N	A	S	G	S	S
P	H	M	J	J	T	J	U	R	H	E	S
K	Q	L	P	B	N	B	Y	J	F	K	O
K	C	O	T	N	I	L	C	M	J	R	N
V	F	C	G	I	L	L	A	R	D	A	G
J	G	G	D	M	R	B	J	J	M	P	F

Abbott
Bowles
Busby
Clement

Francis
Gillard
Givens
Hollins

Leach
Masson
McLintock
Parkes

Sexton
Thomas
Webb

Answers on page 60-61

WORDSEARCH: NOW

Find the words in the grid. Words can go horizontally, vertically and diagonally in all eight directions.

C	F	W	V	J	P	E	J	M	C	R
N	L	U	L	R	I	Y	R	E	H	C
P	I	G	R	K	R	H	E	N	R	Y
D	W	W	C	L	F	V	T	W	M	R
O	G	A	D	B	O	L	T	V	X	E
U	M	D	R	A	U	N	A	H	C	T
G	K	L	J	O	L	H	G	J	N	L
H	J	B	N	G	O	G	C	E	E	O
T	D	G	V	U	V	Z	N	T	E	P
Y	O	K	N	V	H	I	L	L	R	R
G	Y	O	H	Z	F	K	T	T	G	N

Chery   **Gladwin**   **Hill**   **Mackie**
Doughty   **Green**   **Jet**   **Onuoha**
Furlong   **Henry**   **Luongo**   **Polter**

Answers on page 60-61

QPR KIT LAUNCH

QPR unveiled their new kits for the 2015/16 Sky Bet Championship season at Google HQ in London in late June.

R's quartet Nedum Onuoha, Darnell Furlong, Massimo Luongo and Jamie Mackie were all present as the new-look Nike kits were revealed to an audience of Rangers fans and streamed live across QPR's YouTube channel and Google+ page.

Director of Football Les Ferdinand, Head Coach Chris Ramsey and Club Ambassador Andy Sinton were also in attendance.

The home kit features the classic royal blue and white hooped design on the jersey, complemented by a bold, red crew-neck collar. The home kit is completed with all-white shorts and socks.

The away jersey boasts a bold red and black hooped design, accentuated by horizontal royal blue lines. The away kit shorts and socks, like last season, are both black.

The third kit jersey features a unique navy and blue chequered design, which fades from top to bottom. The third kit shorts and socks are both navy.

Nike Dri-FIT technology and engineered

mesh material construction help players stay dry and cool on the pitch. It increases breathability and air flow where athletes need it most, to help the team perform at the highest level.

Mackie, who modelled the home kit, told qpr.co.uk, "I love the new kit, it seems to have gone a bit old school with the thicker hoops and it looks great.

"The QPR kit is always distinctive and I can't wait to wear it for a proper game. I wish pre-season was over and we were in the changing room putting it on for the first match of the season!"

Fellow summer-signing Ben Gladwin, added, "The kits look great.

"From what I've been told the fans prefer the thicker hoops so hopefully they will really like it as well.

"It's down to us as players to try our best now to make it a successful kit for QPR."

STEVE GALLEN'S PRIDE AT PERSONAL PROMOTION

Steve Gallen was confirmed as First Team Coach at QPR earlier this summer after working with the club's younger age groups for the past 18 years.

Gallen, a lifelong R's fan and brother of former captain Kevin, told us that he was "absolutely delighted" when Head Coach Chris Ramsey told him of his new role at the club.

"It was a very proud moment for me and my family," Gallen said.

"I spoke to my parents about it and they were very excited. My cousins, uncles and aunties have all been on the phone, dropping me texts, it's great. We're all big QPR fans in my family so that makes it extra special.

"I have always done my best with whatever age group I was taking, and the hope was to one day work with the first team at QPR.

"I am a big believer in going through the ranks. I have been with schoolboy teams, youth teams, 21s, and this is the next step for me. I am absolutely delighted."

Gallen was at Middlesex University for the start of pre-season training, and he admits the timing of his involvement with the first-team couldn't have been much better.

"In all honesty, any time would have been a great time for it to happen, but it feels really right," he said.

"Seeing so many of the younger lads in the first-team squad, who have come through the ranks, it makes me feel this is a really good time for me to become involved at this level."

Ramsey has made it clear he wants to bring younger players through the system and into the first-team fold, and Gallen is encouraged by what he has seen from the R's gaffer – both from his time at Rangers, and from knowing him before.

"I have full respect for Chris," he said. "When he was working at Tottenham, we used to talk all the time and he is an excellent coach, really hands on, and I'm delighted to be working with him.

"I hope I can help him and act as a bridge between the first team and the academy, having worked for so long with them.

"My job is to help the manager as best I can, and to help the players as best I can. I have been a coach for years and I want to help improve the players. I will be doing everything I can to make the players, Chris and the club successful."

News of Gallen's appointment has proved popular with the R's fans, and he added, "People often say it's important to have QPR people involved with the club and I don't think you'll find too many people who are more QPR than me – although Birchy (Marc Bircham) might have something to say about that!

"I have been a lifelong QPR fan. I know the club, I know the history and I happily tell the lads about it. I think it's important that they know about our football club, and where we have come from.

"Ultimately, it's all about Chris. He has a great feeling for the club and I know that because he has been telling me about it. He wants to be successful and I want to help him achieve that. I'll be doing everything I can."

SIX OF THE SUMMER SO FAR

Here we profile six of the the R's summer signings.

Swindon Duo First Summer Signings

QPR's first two signings of the summer came in the shape of the captures of Ben Gladwin and Massimo Luongo from Swindon Town in early June.

The midfield duo both signed three-year deals.

Luongo, 22, is an Australian international and former Tottenham Hotspur trainee. On signing, he told us, "Regular football is important to me. That's why QPR appealed. I'm at my best when I'm playing week in, week out – I'm all for playing as many games as possible in a season.

"The step up to the Championship is going to be a challenge, but I'll always back myself.

"I sat down with the manager, and a big thing for me was where he wants to go with the club. I was also attracted by how he wanted me to be involved, he sold it to me really well.

"I never want to rest on my laurels – I always want to push on. I'm very excited to now be a QPR player."

Gladwin, also 22, began at Reading before spells in non-league and with Swindon. He added, "I'm really pleased to be joining the club – and I'm really excited.

"There was interest from the Premier League but for me, personally, I think this move is a little more realistic at this stage of my career. Playing is what it's all about. Sitting on the bench is no way to improve your game.

"Chris Ramsey is a fantastic coach and I'm sure he'll improve me on the training pitch. I was hugely impressed by what he had to say and where he sees me fitting in.

"Everyone I've spoken to about QPR said it would be a good move for me. I can't wait to get going here."

Emmanuel-Thomas Jets In

Jay Emmanuel-Thomas became summer signing number three when he joined from Bristol City.

The 24-year-old attacker, also formerly of Arsenal and Ipswich Town, moved to Loftus Road after helping the Robins clinch the League One title last term.

He said, "This is a new chapter for me and I can't wait to get started here.

"As soon as I spoke to Les [Ferdinand] and Chris [Ramsey] and they explained the way they want QPR to play, it was an easy decision for me.

"I'm here to come in and do a job, and I'm confident I can keep improving as a player."

Fans' Favourite Mackie Returns

Crowd favourite Jamie Mackie returned to QPR in mid-June, joining from Nottingham Forest.

The Scottish international forward signed a two-year deal, with the option of a further year.

Mackie played a key role in our promotion to the Premier League in 2010/11, as well as survival the next season, and has returned just two years after leaving for the City Ground.

The 29-year-old, who spent last season on loan at Reading, told us, "I'm absolutely buzzing to be back.

"Anyone who knows me will tell you just how much this club means to me and the feelings that I've got for the place have only grown in the short time I've been away.

"People say never go back, but I feel as though I've got some unfinished business here and under the guidance of Les [Ferdinand] and Chris [Ramsey], I can only see a bright future for this club.

"They know I'll come in and give my absolute maximum and – having in played in front of the QPR fans before – I know that's exactly what they love to see. It's great to be back."

German Front-man Joins R's

QPR secured striker Sebastian Polter from Bundesliga side FSV Mainz 05 at the start of July.

The former Germany Under-21 international, 24, signed a three-year deal at Loftus Road. A former Wolfsburg trainee, Polter spent last season on loan at German second-tier side Union Berlin.

He said, "I'm really happy to be here. It's my dream to play in England, so I couldn't be happier.

"To play for Queens Park Rangers, at this stage of my career, is really good for me and something I am very excited about.

"It's a physical league [the Championship], but I'm a physical player, a team player, and I feel I will adapt.

"I'm really looking forward to playing at Loftus Road in front of the supporters."

QPR Sign Dutch Ace Chery

QPR completed the signing of highly-rated Dutch ace Tjaronn Chery soon after the R's returned from their pre-season training camp in Italy.

The 27-year-old signed a three year deal at Loftus Road, after Rangers activated an undisclosed release clause with FC Groningen for the attacker's services.

Chery became QPR's sixth signing of the summer and his arrival represented a significant coup for the R's, who beat off stiff competition from a number of other clubs to clinch his signature.

An attacking midfielder with an impressive goalscoring record, last season was the most prolific of Chery's career to date, scoring 15 goals in 34 appearances in the Eredivisie.

He is now looking forward to the next chapter of his career in West London, adding, "I am very happy to be here and looking forward to playing for QPR.

"Playing in England has always been a dream of mine and having spoken to Leroy [Fer], he said that QPR is a good fit for me.

"I know the passion of the English fans and how they like to see football played and I can't wait to show what I can do here. It's a really exciting move for me in the best years of my career."

THE MAGIC OF STANLEY BOWLES

When QPR took the old First Division (now the Barclays Premier League) by storm in the early stages of the 1975/76 season, it was widely noted that the west London outfit were a side full of attacking flair.

Dave Sexton's team from Loftus Road was packed full of talent, and at the heart of the magic wearing the famous hooped number 10 shirt was Stanley Bowles, or 'Stan the Man' as he is affectionately known.

That QPR side, arguably the best in the club's history, missed out on the title by a single point to Liverpool. But Stan's brilliance during that campaign in particular helped cement his place in the hearts of the R's faithful, and established him as one of the greatest players and entertainers of the 1970s during the golden age of English football.

Stan set a new goal-scoring record in Europe in 76/77 as Rangers made it to the UEFA Cup Quarter Finals, and he won 5 England caps, netting once. Voted by supporters as QPRs' best-ever player, Stan dazzled fans and opponents alike with his breath-taking talent, his self-confidence and charisma. Along with his off the field antics he has become an icon of the game, a maverick of unmistakeable genius and a legend of Loftus Road!

> **"** I wasn't an arrogant player, but I had so much confidence in my skill, almost a feeling of invincibility. **"**
>
> **STAN BOWLES**

> **"** In terms of playing alongside other players, I think he is one of the finest I've ever known, and I don't say that easily. **"**
>
> **TERRY VENABLES**

> **"** He was easily the best I ever played with. **"**
>
> **GERRY FRANCIS**

> **"** Like watching a player from another era. **"**
>
> **JIMMY GREAVES**

> **"** His tight control, balance, change of pace and cool, clinical finishing stamp him as one of the most talented players I've ever seen. **"**
>
> **DON REVIE**

> **"** Bowles has 100% skill! No one in English football can work a ball better at close quarters. **"**
>
> **DENIS LAW**

> **"** It would be difficult to name any player since the great Stanley Matthews who takes a ball so close to an opponent before beating them. **"**
>
> **DAVE SEXTON**

> **"** I sometimes wondered what all the fuss was about. **"**
>
> **STAN BOWLES**

A BUSY SUMMER IN W12

As well as securing the signatures of a plethora of new players over the summer, Rangers also retained the services of a couple of fans' favourites, and a few of the club's young hopefuls. Here, we look back at a busy few months at Loftus Road.

Over the Hill? Not a Chance!

Fans' favourite Clint Hill signed a new contract at Loftus Road over the summer.

The popular 36-year-old, who joined QPR in the summer of 2010, put pen to paper on a one year extension.

Hill, who has made 170 appearances in all competitions for the R's in the last five years, expressed his excitement about extending his stay in W12 into a sixth year, commenting, "Everyone knows what QPR means to me and I am delighted to be part of the new philosophy that's filtering through the club. It's an exciting time, and there's been a lot of good work done behind the scenes.

"My longevity has surprised me – and it's probably surprised a few others as well. But I've looked after myself well over the years, and I'm still going somehow!

"This season I want to remain fit and put pressure on players that are in the team. I want to set standards in training and prove to myself that I can still do this.

"Professionally, this is the longest I have been at any club and I have thoroughly enjoyed my time here. There have been a few downturns along the way, but as a team and as a club we have always reacted to them and bounced back. I hope we can do the same again this year."

QPR Director of Football, Les Ferdinand, believes Hill still has plenty to offer, telling www.qpr.co.uk, "Clint is a QPR man and the more players you can have on your books that understand what the club is all about, the better.

"He's a fantastic professional who gives everything for the shirt, and we're delighted he's agreed this new deal.

"His influence around the training ground will be invaluable for the existing group of players, but perhaps more importantly for the new players joining us."

Sinton Returns as Club Ambassador

Away from the pitch, QPR also announced the appointment of former QPR winger and England international Andy Sinton as Rangers' first club ambassador.

Sinton, who made 161 league starts for the Hoops during his four-and-a-half-year stay in W12, embarked on his new role in mid-June, working for the club and its charitable arm, QPR in the Community Trust.

In his new role as an ambassador, Sinton's initial duties will include attending matches, working with commercial partners, supporting club-wide events and initiatives, and working closely with the PR, marketing, and community departments to help promote the name of QPR.

"I'm very excited about the new role," Sinton said.

"Ever since I left the club I have always said that I wanted to come back in some capacity at some stage and this feels like a perfect fit, promoting the good name of Queens Park Rangers Football Club across a variety of mediums.

"Football is everything I know and love and to stay involved in the game is fantastic. To do that at QPR, where I enjoyed the best years of my career, is even better.

There's Only Two Furlongs

Darnell Furlong put pen to paper on a new two-year contract earlier this summer, joining a host of QPR youngsters who extended their stay at Loftus Road.

It capped a breakthrough season for the 19-year-old, son of R's legend and Under-18s boss Paul, after making his Premier League debut in February. The full-back lasted the full 90 minutes at Hull City before repeating the feat on home soil against Arsenal 11 days later.

He was also voted the EDS Young Player of the Year by R's fans following his breakthrough season.

Furlong, former Youth Team captain, has been at Rangers since the age of 10 and will remain in W12 until the summer of 2017.

Furlong was one of several Under-21s to commit their immediate futures to the club, with goalkeeper Joe Lumley also agreeing a new two-year deal.

"I've always had a good relationship with the fans, on and off the field, better than anywhere else I played, so to work closely with them again in the community and on matchdays is going to be an amazing experience for me.

"It's going to be an absolute pleasure and a privilege."

QPR Co-Chairman, Tony Fernandes, added, "This is a really important appointment.

"Andy is one of a number of former players who share a great affiliation with QPR and utilising him across all areas of the club to promote what we do is a massive step in the right direction for us.

"It's important that he gets out in the community and shows what QPR is – a family football club.

"He is a vibrant, infectious personality and I am sure he will flourish in this role.

"With Andy and Les back at QPR, we now have people with very deep roots in the club, which we as a board deem hugely important."

"I'm extremely happy," Faurlin said.

"I have to say thank you to everyone at the club for keeping me here and giving me the chance to prove a lot of people wrong. I just want to play football.

"I contemplated giving up after my last injury. It was really tough and I was in a dark place. Thankfully, I'm still here.

"All you can do is give your best to come back. The support from everyone in and around the club has been massive and I am eternally grateful for that.

"I have trained with the lads for three to four months now. I feel confident. I'm ready to go again.

"I can't wait to play in front of the QPR fans. I feel part of the family, I have done for six years.

"I'm sure next season is going to be a good one. I love this place."

QPR's Director of Football, Les Ferdinand, added, "Everyone knows what Ale means to QPR and what QPR means to Ale, but there was no sentiment involved here.

"The way he fought back from his injury last season is all credit to him and he showed what a talented player he is on the training ground during the final few weeks of last season.

"If he can stay fit, which we really hope he can, he will be a big asset for us in the coming season.

"We're delighted he's agreed a new deal with the club."

Argie Ace Pens New Deal

Alejandro Faurlin agreed a new deal at Loftus Road this summer.

The 28-year-old Argentine midfielder put pen to paper on a one-year contact with the option of a further year.

Faurlin, who initially joined QPR in July 2009, missed the majority of last season owing to a third ACL injury in as many years, but having fought back to fitness in the latter stages of the campaign, he's now relishing the chance to prove his worth once again after signing a new deal.

KNOW YOUR R'SSS!

How well do you know your favourite Super-Hoops stars? Below are eight of the current first team squad but we've disguised them to make it tricky to identify them. How many can you name?

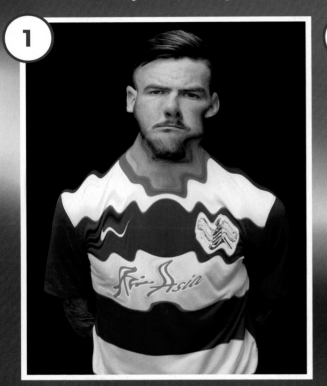

1

2

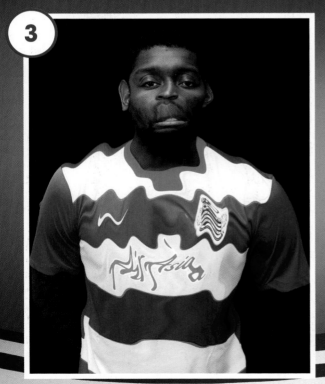

3

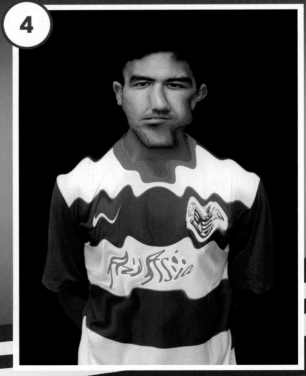

4

5

6

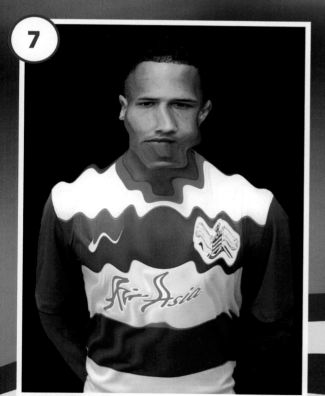

7

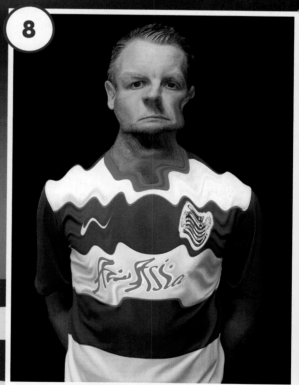

8

Answers on page 60-61

QUIZ ANSWERS

Page 13 – Spot the ball: Answer C

Page 38 – Wordsearch

S	A	D	W	N	O	T	X	E	S	L	K
N	B	Y	R	E	X	B	S	N	E	L	C
E	B	K	S	N	B	N	O	A	N	L	Q
V	O	W	R	I	I	B	C	W	E	T	R
I	T	K	D	L	C	H	Z	M	L	Y	M
G	T	G	L	K	X	N	E	N	B	E	A
T	H	O	M	A	S	N	A	S	G	S	S
P	H	M	J	J	T	J	U	R	H	E	S
K	Q	L	P	B	N	B	Y	J	F	K	O
K	C	O	T	N	I	L	C	M	J	R	N
V	F	C	G	I	L	L	A	R	D	A	G
J	G	G	D	M	R	B	J	J	M	P	F

Page 39 – Wordsearch

C	F	W	V	J	P	E	J	M	C	R
N	L	U	L	R	I	Y	R	E	H	C
P	I	G	R	K	R	H	E	N	R	Y
D	W	W	C	L	F	V	T	W	M	R
O	G	A	D	B	O	L	T	V	X	E
U	M	D	R	A	U	N	A	H	C	T
G	K	L	J	O	L	H	G	J	N	L
H	J	B	N	G	O	G	C	E	E	O
T	D	G	V	U	V	Z	N	T	E	P
Y	O	K	N	V	H	I	L	L	R	R
G	Y	O	H	Z	F	K	T	T	G	N

Page 26 – Quiz Part One

1. Charlie Austin, 18
2. Mauricio Isla and Eduardo Vargas
3. 3
4. Charlie Austin
5. Sunderland, 1-0
6. Rob Green
7. Matt Phillips
8. Rio Ferdinand, number 5
9. Leroy Fer, the Netherlands
10. Chris Ramsey
11. 12
12. Charlie Austin, scored 3 and missed 2
13. 3
14. The number 9 shirt, Les Ferdinand
15. Manchester United
16. Darnell Furlong, Hull City
17. 42
18. 4.1 away to West Brom.
19. Scotland
20. Niko Kranjkar

Page 34 – Quiz Part Two

1. 1967 League Cup Final and 2003 Play-off Final
2. Dark blue and light blue halves
3. Green and white
4. 1982 and 1987
5. Red tops, black shorts and socks
6. Le coq sportif
7. Clubhouse
8. He is wearing an Umbro top and Adidas shorts and socks
9. Umbro
10. Adidas
11. Holland Fly KLM, Air Asia, Air Malaysia, Gulf Air
12. 1927
13. Admiral
14. Ericsson
15. Classic FM
16. Orange
17. 13
18. 3
19. Green and white
20. 1982, Guinness

Page 58 – Know your R'sss!

1 Ben Gladwin

2 Yun Suk Young

3 Jay Emmanuel Thomas

4 Massimo Luongo

5 Karl Henry

6 Sebastian Polter

7 Tjarronn Chery

8 Clint Hill

WHERE'S THE GAFFER?

Can you find Chris Ramsey in the crowd?